CECIL'S PRIDE
THE TRUE STORY OF A LION KING

TOLD BY CRAIG HATKOFF, JULIANA HATKOFF, AND ISABELLA HATKOFF
PHOTOGRAPHS BY BRENT STAPELKAMP

SCHOLASTIC INC.

Brent Stapelkamp's last photo of Cecil, taken May 27, 2015.

We dedicate this book to all the organizations and people on the ground who fight to protect our planet every day, and to Cecil, whose story has awakened the world from a deep and dangerous slumber just in time.

Library of Congress Cataloging-in-Publication Data is available.

ISBN 978-1-338-03445-5

10 9 8 7 6 5 4 3 2 1   16 17 18 19 20

Printed in the U.S.A.   88 · First edition, May 2016

Book design by Jessica Meltzer · The text was set in Adobe Garamond

We would like to thank Brent Stapelkamp, Rachel Mandel, Meredith Cohen, Brenda Kosara, Elizabeth Herzog, Debra Dorfman, Ellie Berger, and our mom, Jane Rosenthal, for her ongoing support.

For more information about our growing collection of true animal stories, please visit www.owenandmzee.com, www.knut.net, www.miza.com, www.winterstail.com, and www.cecil.org.

To Our Readers,

We are proud to share the true story of Cecil the Lion seen through the lens of his real-life "keeper," Brent Stapelkamp. For nine years, Brent, a wildlife researcher from Oxford University, tracked and documented Cecil's every move while beautifully photographing his life. As Brent explained Cecil's extraordinary family history to us, it became clear. Everyone knew how Cecil died. We would tell the story of how Cecil lived.

In the wild, lions must fight to defend their pride and their territory against other lions who challenge them. Remarkably, several years ago Cecil and his longtime challenger and archrival, Jericho, decided to join forces, forming an improbable alliance—something rarely seen between lions of different bloodlines. After Cecil's death, Brent and his fellow researchers feared Jericho would follow nature's normal call, abandoning Cecil's cubs to start his own family. Jericho surprised them all, rising to the occasion and taking in Cecil's cubs as his own. It seems Cecil had yet another keeper.

An outpouring of grief and anger from the hunting down of one majestic black-mane lion had started a global conversation about individual and collective responsibility to protect our animals and our planet. But amidst the tragedy emerged a powerful lesson. We are all our brother's keeper. Come celebrate the life of a real Lion King. We hope you enjoy the story of **Cecil's Pride.**

With love and peace,

Craig Hatkoff   Juliana Hatkoff   Isabella Hatkoff

LIONS HAVE always been a symbol of strength and courage. They are known as the king of beasts, but only one lion king became known by everyone. His name was Cecil.

Cecil ruled a very large territory in Africa inside Hwange National Park, Zimbabwe's largest game reserve. About the size of the state of Connecticut, the park is even larger than many countries. Thousands of people visit Hwange every year to see the wildlife and take photographs. Cecil was well known because he seemed to enjoy having his picture taken by tourists. Unlike most of the animals, he would casually stroll by the safari vehicles and pose.

Lions aren't the only animals that call Hwange home. Giraffes, zebras, elephants, leopards, and rhinos roam freely through the vast deserts, forests, and grasslands. There are no fences or walls like in a zoo.

Hwange has a diverse ecosystem, but there's a delicate balance. When something changes, it can send a ripple throughout the whole park. No one knew it yet, but a giant ripple was about to travel around the globe.

Cecil the king.

On a typical day in Hwange National Park, dozens of safari guides drive tourists around the property in the hope of seeing wild animals in their natural environment. The safari guides never know exactly where the animals will be, but they are really good at finding them. For example, they know that a pan—or natural watering hole—is a place where animals like to gather when they're thirsty.

But Brent Stapelkamp has a different way of finding animals. As a lion researcher, he is able to put a GPS tracking collar on an animal. Brent can check his electronic tracking equipment and computer to see the animal's location and study its behaviors. He can often be seen holding up an aluminum antenna, trying to get a signal.

Brent uses the data he collects to develop plans for conservation. His goal was to figure out how much land would be necessary to support the lion population in the future.

Brent can recognize individual lions by their unique patterns of whisker spots. Each pattern is different, like a human fingerprint. Only the really memorable lions get names—and Cecil was one of those lions.

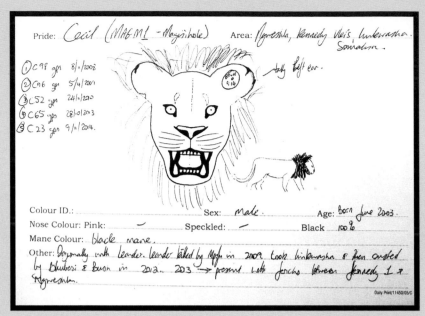

Cecil's whisker print hand-drawn by Brent.

Cecil was the leader of a pride, which is a family of 15 or more lions and cubs. He was easy to identify because of his large size, his dramatic black mane, and Brent's tracking collar.

Before Cecil became king, he and his brother Leander left their pride at the age of about five and took over an area of Hwange National Park called the Ngweshla Pan.

It was the best place for lions to live because there was plenty of water to drink all year round and plenty of animals to eat, like zebras and wildebeest. Other lions wanted to live there, too. Even though lions are social animals, they need their own large territory to hunt, mate, and live. They don't share their territory with other prides. Only one group of lions can rule an area at a time.

Cecil's bold, black mane made him instantly recognizable.

In 2009, one of the strongest lions in the park challenged Cecil. His name was Mpofu, and he wanted to take over Ngweshla. Cecil and Leander fought back as best they could. They wounded Mpofu so badly that he ran away. But unfortunately, Mpofu had hurt Cecil's brother even more. Sadly, Leander didn't survive the fight. Cecil was now a lion on his own.

Mpofu had three sons named Jericho, Judah, and Job. Hearing the fight, Mpofu's sons raced over and found that Cecil had attacked their father. Mpofu's son Jericho charged after Cecil. Without Leander, Cecil wasn't strong enough to hold his position. He retreated. With Cecil gone, Jericho and his two brothers could take over Ngweshla.

Years went by before Cecil and Jericho would cross paths with each other again.

top left: Mpofu; top right: Jericho; bottom left: Judah; bottom right: Job

Cecil found a new area of Hwange to settle in called Linkwasha. Jericho became the leader of a pride in Ngweshla. Both lions were about to be challenged again by a pair of brothers.

The lion brothers entered Cecil's territory first. It was two-on-one, and the brothers were stronger. Cecil ran away. Then the brothers moved on and forced Jericho out of his territory and away from his pride.

Now Cecil and Jericho were on the run. As the two rivals roamed around the park, they eventually crossed paths. It was 2013, and it had been three years since they last saw each other. They roared. They crouched. They fought.

Brent had been watching and tracking Cecil and Jericho as part of his research. He knew Cecil had fought Jericho's father, and that Jericho's father had attacked Cecil's brother. *This is not going to end well*, he thought.

Cecil and Jericho fight for control of their territory.

Cecil approaching Jericho.

But then something changed. A few days later, Brent got a call from a safari lodge. "Cecil and Jericho are together!" they said. Brent couldn't believe it. The fighting had unexpectedly transformed into a partnership.

Cecil and Jericho were stronger as a team. It is extremely rare that two unrelated male lions could live together in the same territory. For reasons we do not fully comprehend, Cecil and Jericho came to their own understanding. Together, they could take over more land, including the land they once ruled. As allies, Cecil and Jericho could survive.

Prior to coming together, Cecil and Jericho had each formed their own pride, filled with lionesses and cubs. Black manes tend to attract lionesses, by signaling their strength and health, while intimidating other male lions. The prides stayed together for safety, and to help one another defend the territory. As a group, they could share food, water, and shelter.

No one could have predicted that Cecil (bottom) and Jericho (top) would form an alliance.

Cecil's lionesses sharing a sweet moment.

One of Cecil's cubs practicing his roar.

Cecil had fathered eight cubs by the time he was 13 years old. Cubs are born helpless and blind. They don't even learn to hunt until they're at least a year old. It was Cecil's duty to protect his cubs from harm. If left on their own, they could easily be attacked by hyenas or leopards.

Lionesses are in charge of feeding the family, which means they do most of the hunting. They're smaller and faster than male lions, and can run the length of a football field in just five seconds. But eating is a family activity. As the leader of the pride, Cecil got the first bite.

One day, Brent captured a photo of Cecil and his family feasting on an elephant. Once Cecil had his fill, he took a nap, resting his head right on the elephant's body. With his entire family surrounding him—more than 20 lions and cubs—he looked peaceful and happy.

Cecil and a lioness.

Even though Hwange National Park is a protected area that keeps animals safe from hunters, there are no physical boundaries to prevent lions from wandering off the property and into an area where hunting might be legal.

In early July 2015, Cecil caught a whiff of a scent—dinner. To follow the scent, he had to cross the train tracks and exit Hwange National Park. A meal for his family was not to be ignored. It was dark out. Following the scent, he crossed over the tracks.

When he got to the other side, there was no prey in sight. The scent had been planted by lion hunters. Cecil didn't know it, but he had walked right into a trap. The hunter became the hunted.

A few days later, Brent realized the tracking device on Cecil had stopped working near the train tracks. He called the park rangers before he traveled to Hwange. He knew he wouldn't like what he found.

A commanding Cecil roaming through Hwange.

Brent couldn't believe that Cecil was gone, but his thoughts quickly turned to Cecil's pride. What would happen to Cecil's cubs?

Another male lion would step in and take over as the leader. Would it be Jericho? Regardless of who it was, any new pride leader would most likely want to start a new family with new cubs, which means he'd attack the existing cubs. Brent knew Cecil's cubs were less than a year old and would never survive on their own.

Brent had lost Cecil, and he didn't want to lose Cecil's cubs, too. He feared for what would happen next. But there was another problem: No one could find Jericho.

Cecil's cubs found alive and well following his passing.

Jericho hadn't been seen for days. Park employees found his tracks in the dirt, but they couldn't catch a glimpse of Cecil's former rival. *He must be roaming the park and searching for Cecil,* they thought. Finally, Brent and the park employees heard him.

Near the train tracks, Jericho was making a quiet grumbling noise calling out to Cecil so as not to attract rival lions who might detect weakness. He waited for a reply but never got one. Jericho was now alone. He headed back toward the pride, to take over as the new king of the jungle.

Jericho reappears as the new lion king gazing over his territory.

Jericho and his playful cubs.

Brent was relieved to find Jericho, but he was more anxious about what Jericho would do to Cecil's cubs. Soon after Jericho returned as leader of the pride, he also became the protector of Cecil's cubs.

Jericho had surprised Brent yet again. The new king unexpectedly accepted Cecil's cubs as his own. Their prospects for survival were strong, and Brent believed they had an excellent chance of living to become the next generation of the king of beasts.

Brent still studies Cecil's cubs in the park, and he sees that they seem happy and well fed. He's found them playing among elephants with Jericho watching nearby. Cecil is no longer with us, but his legacy lives on, thanks to an incredible partnership with an unlikely friend.

Jericho and Cathy, a lioness, camouflaged within the grasslands.

Most days, the dusty plains of Hwange teem with life dancing to the sounds of nature's orchestra. A silence fell upon Hwange and the world as a hunter's arrow felled a single lion. Then, from the anger and despair, a mighty roar began across the globe, asking new questions, seeking answers, and imposing new laws and regulations not only about the illegal hunting of lions, but other endangered species as well. US lawmakers even proposed the Conserving Ecosystems by Ceasing the Importation of Large Animal Trophies (CECIL) Act, among others.

The whole world knows how Cecil died. We hope *Cecil's Pride*, the story of how Cecil lived, helps paint a fuller picture and creates a cause for celebration worthy of a true lion king. Cecil's remaining pride, his living legacy, now under the protection of Jericho, helps illuminate for us important lessons, old and new. We are all our brothers' keeper. And out of tragedy and darkness, a new king shall always arise.

Cecil photographed with a distant stare.

FACTS ABOUT LIONS

■ Unlike other species, lions are very social creatures. They're the only cats that live in prides, or large groups. Prides are often made of one to three males, about a dozen females, and all of their cubs. Since almost everyone is related to one another, the prides have a tight bond, just like a family.

■ Lions are fiercely protective of their prides and their territories. If a new leader takes over, it's often by force, as both Jericho and Cecil experienced in the past. What's unique about Cecil and Jericho's story is that it's unusual for cubs to survive the changing of the guard. The new leader of a pride wants to continue his bloodline, so he often kills the existing cubs that are less than one year old. Almost 70 percent of lion cubs die before they reach adulthood because they are killed or from starvation or disease.

GLOBAL IMPACT OF CECIL'S DEATH

Cecil's death attracted a lot of attention around the world, and spurred many discussions about the illegal hunting, or poaching, of animals and conservation efforts in Africa.

Some animals are hunted legally in Africa, including lions, buffaloes, elephants, and leopards. Some argue that these expeditions, often called "trophy hunting," can help fund conservation efforts when managed properly. Hunting tourism is a crucial source of income in Africa. Traditional tourism doesn't currently cover all of the expenses surrounding national parks, game reserves, conservation, and anti-poaching education.

Oxford University lion researcher Brent Stapelkamp doesn't believe all hunting should be banished—just lion hunting. Like we saw with Cecil, lions are social creatures and the loss of a leader is felt deeply throughout the pride. Hunting for sport could alter behaviors, change the balance of male to female lions, and result in an increase in cub deaths as the leaders of prides are hunted.

The lion species could soon become endangered. About 30,000 lions used to roam Africa freely a decade ago, but now it's estimated that only 20,000 lions remain. The Wildlife Conservation Research Unit says lions are killed daily, and that illegal hunting is a threat to the species' survival. The decreasing numbers can also be attributed to a decrease in prey and habitat loss.

Cecil's photo was projected onto the Empire State Building as part of the Oceanic Preservation Society's effort to raise awareness for the world's endangered animals in August 2015.

HWANGE NATIONAL PARK

Hwange National Park is Zimbabwe's largest game reserve. It's located just one hour away from the world's largest waterfall, Victoria Falls.

It's been a national park since 1929, and now tourists from around the world visit each year to admire over 100 species of mammals and 400 species of birds. The park is known for its elephant population, which is one of the largest in the world.

You can visit Hwange National Park on safari and see Cecil's home for yourself. Day and night, guides take visitors on drives or walking safaris. Although the park is now missing its famed resident, a conservation group plans to build a statue in honor of Cecil the Lion at the park's entrance.

OXFORD UNIVERSITY STUDY

Cecil the Lion was studied from 2008 to 2015 by researchers like Brent Stapelkamp at the University of Oxford's Wildlife Conservation Research Unit (WildCRU). Cecil was collared at age five for the Hwange Lion Project.

In partnership with big cat scientists at Panthera, a conservation organization, WildCRU works with governments, park managers, and local communities to develop actionable solutions that help protect and conserve lions.

Researchers have been learning much from the behavior of lions like Cecil, especially when it comes to their roaming patterns and distances. Some GPS-collared lions in the study live in an astounding 116-square-mile area. This information is important in predicting how much land will be required for future conservation efforts.